The
Kabir
Book

Other Books by Robert Bly

The Kabir Book

Forty-Four
of the
Ecstatic
Poems of
Kabir

Versions
by
Robert Bly

A Seventies Press Book
Beacon Press–Boston

Copyright © 1971, 1977 by Robert Bly
Copyright © 1977 by The Seventies Press

Beacon Press books are published under the auspices
of the Unitarian Universalist Association

Published simultaneously in hardcover and paperback editions

Simultaneous publication in Canada
by Fitzhenry & Whiteside, Ltd., Toronto

Printed in the United States of America

(hardcover)   9   8   7   6   5   4   3   2   1
(paperback)   9   8   7   6   5   4   3   2   1

Library of Congress Cataloging in Publication Data

Kabir, 15th cent.
  The Kabir book.
  "A Seventies Press book."
  I. Bly, Robert.   II. Title.
PK2095.K3K32   1977   891.43'1'2   76–7737
ISBN 0–8070–6378–9
ISBN 0–8070–6379–7 (pbk.)

Grateful acknowledgment is made to Macmillan Publishing Co., Inc. (New York),
and to Macmillan Ltd (London and Basingstoke), for permission to reprint the first
line of LIII by Rabindranath Tagore from *Songs of Kabir* and to rephrase selections from
the same book. From *Songs of Kabir* by Rabindranath Tagore, Copyright 1915 by
Macmillan Publishing Co., Inc., renewed 1942 by Rabindranath Tagore, Trustees of
the Tagore Estate, and Macmillan (London and Basingstoke).

*Dedicated to Kabir, and all those working
confused in inner labor*

*Rumi says: Ecstatic love is an ocean, and the Milky Way
is a flake of foam floating on it.*

Acknowledgments

Thanks to the editors of the following magazines, in which these poems appeared:
Garrett, Greensboro Review, Kaleidoscope, Kamadhenu, Lillabulero, New Work, East West Journal, Blackstone Press Postcard, Boundary, La Booche Review, Rawa Journal, Lower Stumpf Lake Review, Paris Review, Street Magazine, Ally Press, WIN, Hawaii Review, Cold Mountain Press Postcard, Kayak, Slow Loris Press Broadsides. And to *Rainbow Bridge Books* who have kept the booklet, "The fish in the sea is not thirsty," in which these poems appeared, in print.

Also thanks to the *Ally Press* for printing 20 poems in the second group.

A special thanks to David Sykes, who did the design for the *Lillabulero* edition, and to Karyl Klopp, who designed this edition.

This Book Has Three Groups of Poems

The Fish in the Sea Is Not Thirsty

The Bhakti Path

The Only Woman Awake
Is the Woman Who
Has Heard the Flute

These are poems by Kabir, the fifteenth-century Indian. He was the son of a Moslem weaver in Benares, but his spiritual growth was influenced by Sufi poets and the ideas of the Hindus. You can read about him in *One Hundred Poems of Kabir*, translated by Rabindranath Tagore, assisted by Evelyn Underhill (Macmillan), still in print. The English of the Tagore-Underhill translations is hopeless, and I simply put a few of them, whose interiors I had become especially fond of, into more contemporary language, to see what they might look like. In one poem I violated chronology, putting "a loaded gun" where Tagore says "deadly weapon." I noticed that we have defenses against the general and the nostalgic, but not against the specific and the contemporary. That doesn't excuse the change, but explains my motive. I believe in translation being as accurate as possible. Kabir wrote the originals in Hindi; Tagore was working from a Bengali translation of that. Many errors may be built in. If anyone speaking Hindi would like to help me, I'll do them over.

The Fish in the Sea Is Not Thirsty

1

When my friend is away from me, I am
depressed;
nothing in the daylight delights me,
sleep at night gives no rest,
who can I tell about this?

The night is dark, and long . . . hours go by . . .
because I am alone, I sit up suddenly,
fear goes through me. . . .

Kabir says: Listen, my friend
there is one thing in the world that satisfies,
and that is a meeting with the Guest.

2

I don't know what sort of a God we have been talking about.

The caller calls in a loud voice to the Holy One at dusk.
Why? Surely the Holy One is not deaf.
He hears the delicate anklets that ring on the feet of an insect as it walks.

Go over and over your beads, paint weird designs on your forehead,
wear your hair matted, long, and ostentatious,
but when deep inside you there is a loaded gun, how can you have God?

3

Oh friend, I love you, think this over
carefully! If you are in love,
then why are you asleep?

If you have found him,
give yourself to him, take him.

Why do you lose track of him again and again?

If you are about to fall into heavy sleep anyway,
why waste time smoothing the bed
and arranging the pillows?

Kabir will tell you the truth: this is what love is like:
suppose you had to cut your head off
and give it to someone else,
what difference would that make?

4

Student, do the simple purification.

You know that the seed is inside the horse-chestnut
    tree;
and inside the seed there are the blossoms of the tree,
    and the chestnuts, and the shade.
So inside the human body there is the seed, and
    inside the seed there is the human body again.

Fire, air, earth, water, and space — if you don't want
    the secret one,
you can't have these either.

Thinkers, listen, tell me what you know of that is not
    inside the soul?
Take a pitcher full of water and set it down on the
    water —
now it has water inside and water outside.
We mustn't give it a name,
lest silly people start talking again about the body and
    the soul.

If you want the truth, I'll tell you the truth:
Listen to the secret sound, the real sound, which is
    inside you.
The one no one talks of speaks the secret sound to
    himself,
and he is the one who has made it all.

5

Inside this clay jug there are canyons and pine
mountains, and the maker of canyons and pine
mountains!
All seven oceans are inside, and hundreds of millions
of stars.
The acid that tests gold is there, and the one who
judges jewels.
And the music from the strings no one touches, and
the source of all water.

If you want the truth, I will tell you the truth:
Friend, listen: the God whom I love is inside.

6

W hy should we two ever want to part?

Just as the leaf of the water rhubarb lives floating on
the water,
we live as the great one and little one.

As the owl opens his eyes all night to the moon,
we live as the great one and little one.

This love between us goes back to the first humans;
it cannot *be* annihilated.

Here is Kabir's idea: as the river gives itself into the
ocean,
what is inside me moves inside you.

7

Why should I flail about with words, when love
has made the space inside me full of light?
I know the diamond is wrapped in this cloth, so why
should I open it all the time and look?
When the pan was empty, it flew up; now that it's
full, why bother weighing it?

The swan has flown to the mountain lake!
Why bother with ditches and holes any more?
The Holy One lives inside you —
why open your other eyes at all?

Kabir will tell you the truth: Listen, brother!
The Guest, who makes my eyes so bright,
has made love with me.

8

I laugh when I hear that the fish in the water is
thirsty.

You don't grasp the fact that what is most alive of all
is inside your own house;
and so you walk from one holy city to the next with a
confused look!

Kabir will tell you the truth: go wherever you like, to
Calcutta or Tibet;
if you can't find where your soul is hidden,
for you the world will never be real!

9

Knowing nothing shuts the iron gates; the new love opens them.

The sound of the gates opening wakes the beautiful woman asleep.

Kabir says: Fantastic! Don't let a chance like this go by!

10

Between the conscious and the unconscious, the
mind has put up a swing:
all earth creatures, even the supernovas, sway
    between these two trees,
and it never winds down.

Angels, animals, humans, insects by the million, also
    the wheeling sun and moon;
ages go by, and it goes on.

Everything is swinging: heaven, earth, water, fire,
and the secret one slowly growing a body.
Kabir saw that for fifteen seconds, and it made him a
    servant for life.

11

My inside, listen to me, the greatest spirit,
the Teacher, is near,
wake up, wake up!

Run to his feet —
he is standing close to your head right now.

You have slept for millions and millions of years.

Why not wake up this morning?

12

There is a flag no one sees blowing in the
sky-temple.
A blue cloth has been stretched up,
it is decorated with the moon and many jewels.

The sun and the moon can be seen in that place;
when looking at that, bring your mind down to
silence.

I will tell you the truth:
the man who has drunk from that liquid wanders
around like someone insane.

13

There's a moon in my body, but I can't see it!
A moon and a sun.
A drum never touched by hands, beating, and I can't
hear it!

As long as a human being worries about when he will
die, and what he has that is his,
all of his works are zero.
When affection for the I-creature and what it owns is
dead,
then the work of the Teacher is over.

The purpose of labor is to learn;
when you know it, the labor is over.
The apple blossom exists to create fruit; when that
comes, the petals fall.

The musk is inside the deer, but the deer does not
look for it:
it wanders around looking for grass.

16

14

I said to the wanting-creature inside me:
What is this river you want to cross?
There are no travelers on the river-road, and no road.
Do you see anyone moving about on that bank, or
    resting?
There is no river at all, and no boat, and no boatman.
There is no towrope either, and no one to pull it.
There is no ground, no sky, no time, no bank, no
    ford!

And there is no body, and no mind!
Do you believe there is some place that will make the
    soul less thirsty?
In that great absence you will find nothing.

Be strong then, and enter into your own body;
there you have a solid place for your feet.
Think about it carefully!
Don't go off somewhere else!

Kabir says this: just throw away all thoughts of
    imaginary things,
and stand firm in that which you are.

18

The Bhakti Path

15

My body and my mind are in depression because you are not with me.

How much I love you and want you in my house!

When I hear people describe me as your bride I look sideways ashamed,

because I know that far inside us we have never met.

Then what is this love of mine?

I don't really care about food, I don't really care about sleep,

I am restless indoors and outdoors.

The bride wants her lover as much as a thirsty man wants water.

And how will I find someone who will take a message to the Guest from me?

How restless Kabir is all the time!

How much he wants to see the Guest!

16

The flute of interior time is played whether we
  hear it or not,
What we mean by "love" is its sound coming in.
When love hits the farthest edge of excess, it reaches
    a wisdom.
And the fragrance of that knowledge!
It penetrates our thick bodies,
it goes through walls —
Its network of notes has a structure as if a million
    suns were arranged inside.
This tune has truth in it.
Where else have you heard a sound like this?

17

What comes out of the harp? Music!
And there is a dance no hands or feet dance.
No fingers play it, no ears hear it,
because the Holy One is the ear,
and the one listening too.

The great doors remain closed, but the spring
fragrance
comes inside anyway,
and no one sees what takes place there.
Men and women who have entered through both
doors at once will understand this poem.

18

I talk to my inner lover, and I say, why such rush?
We sense that there is some sort of spirit that loves
    birds and animals and the ants —
perhaps the same one who gave a radiance to you in
    your mother's womb.
Is it logical you would be walking around entirely
    orphaned now?
The truth is you turned away yourself,
and decided to go into the dark alone.
Now you are tangled up in others, and have forgotten
    what you once knew,
and that's why everything you do has some weird
    failure in it.

19

Friend, hope for the Guest while you are alive.
Jump into experience while you are alive!
Think . . . and think . . . while you are alive.
What you call "salvation" belongs to the time before
    death.

If you don't break your ropes while you're alive,
do you think
ghosts will do it after?

The idea that the soul will join with the ecstatic
just because the body is rotten —
that is all fantasy.
What is found now is found then.
If you find nothing now,
you will simply end up with an apartment in the City
    of Death.
If you make love with the divine now, in the next life
    you will have the face of satisfied desire.

So plunge into the truth, find out who the Teacher is,
    Believe in the Great Sound!

Kabir says this: When the Guest is being searched for,
   it is the intensity of the longing for the Guest that
   does all the work.
Look at me, and you will see a slave of that intensity.

20

I know the sound of the ecstatic flute,
but I don't know whose flute it is.

A lamp burns and has neither wick nor oil.

A lily pad blossoms and is not attached to the bottom!

When one flower opens, ordinarily dozens open.

The moon bird's head is filled with nothing but
    thoughts of the moon,
and when the next rain will come is all that the rain
    bird thinks of.

Who is it we spend our entire life loving?

21

What has death and a thick body dances before what has no thick body and no death.

The trumpet says: "I am you."

The spiritual master arrives and bows down to the beginning student.

Try to live to see this!

22

I have been thinking of the difference
between water
and the waves on it. Rising,
water's still water, falling back,
it is water, will you give me a hint
how to tell them apart?

Because someone has made up the word
"wave," do I have to distinguish it
from water?

There is a Secret One inside us;
the planets in all the galaxies
pass through his hands like beads.

That is a string of beads one should look at with
luminous eyes.

23

The bhakti path winds in a delicate way.
On this path there is no asking and no not asking.
The ego simply disappears the moment you touch
   him.
The joy of looking for him is so immense that you
   just dive in,
and coast around like a fish in the water.
If anyone needs a head, the lover leaps up to offer
   his.
Kabir's poems touch on the secrets of this bhakti.

24

Let's leave for the country where the Guest lives!
There the water jar is filling with water
even though there is no rope to lower it.
There the skies are always blue,
and yet rain falls on the earth.
Do you have a body? Don't sit on the porch!
Go out and walk in the rain!
The fall moon rides the sky all month there,
and it would sound silly to mention only one sun —
the light there comes from a number of them.

25

Are you looking for me? I am in the next seat.
My shoulder is against yours.
You will not find me in stupas, not in Indian shrine
rooms, nor in synagogues, nor in cathedrals:
not in masses, nor kirtans, not in legs winding
around your own neck, nor in eating nothing but
vegetables.
When you really look for me, you will see me
instantly —
you will find me in the tiniest house of time.
Kabir says: Student, tell me, what is God?
He is the breath inside the breath.

26

The darkness of night is coming along fast, and
the shadows of love close in the body and
the mind.
Open the window to the west, and disappear into the
air inside you.

Near your breastbone there is an open flower.
Drink the honey that is all around that flower.
Waves are coming in:
there is so much magnificence near the ocean!
Listen: Sound of big seashells! Sound of bells!

Kabir says: Friend, listen, this is what I have to say:
The Guest I love is inside me!

27

It is time to put up a love-swing!
Tie the body and then tie the mind so that they
    swing between the arms of the Secret One you
    love,
Bring the water that falls from the clouds to your
    eyes,
and cover yourself inside entirely with the shadow of
    night.
Bring your face up close to his ear,
and then talk only about what you want deeply to
    happen.
Kabir says: Listen to me, brother, bring the shape,
    face, and odor of the Holy One inside you.

28

There is nothing but water in the holy pools.
I know, I have been swimming in them.
All the gods sculpted of wood or ivory can't say a
   word.
I know, I have been crying out to them.
The Sacred Books of the East are nothing but words.
I looked through their covers one day sideways.
What Kabir talks of is only what he has lived
   through.
If you have not lived through something, it is not
   true.

The Only Woman Awake
Is the Woman Who
Has Heard the Flute

29

Clouds grow heavy; thunder goes.
   Rain drives in from the east, its patter falls on
   the sides of houses.
Rain can be destructive, wiping out boundary marks.
But the soil needs care — ecstatic love has sprouts,
   now, and renunciation.
Let the rain feed both.
Only the farmer with intelligence actually brings his
   harvest back to his farmyard.
He will fill the granary bins, and feed both the wise
   men and the saints.

30

Friend, wake up! Why do you go on sleeping?
    The night is over — do you want to lose the day
    the same way?
Other women who managed to get up early have
    already found an elephant or a jewel. . . .
So much was lost already while you slept . . .
and that was so unnecessary!

The one who loves you understood, but you did not.
You forgot to make a place in your bed next to you.
Instead you spent your life playing.
In your twenties you did not grow
because you did not know who your Lord was.
Wake up! Wake up! There's no one in your bed —
He left you during the long night.

Kabir says: The only woman awake is the woman
    who has heard the flute!

31

I played for ten years with the girls my own age,
but now I am suddenly in fear.
I am on the way up some stairs — they are high.
Yet I have to give up my fears
if I want to take part in this love.

I have to let go the protective clothes
and meet him with the whole length of my body.
My eyes will have to be the love-candles this time.
Kabir says: Men and women in love will understand
this poem.
If what you feel for the Holy One is not desire,
then what's the use of dressing with such care,
and spending so much time making your eyelids
dark?

32

I married my Lord, and meant to live with him.
But I did not live with him, I turned away,
and all at once my twenties were gone.

The night I was married all my friends sang for me,
and the rice of pleasure and the rice of pain fell
on me.

Yet when all those ceremonies were over, I left, I did
not go home with him,
and my relatives all the way home said, "It's all
right."

Kabir says: Now my love energy is actually mine.
This time I will take it with me when I go,
and outside his house I will blow the horn of
triumph!

33

The small ruby everyone wants has fallen out on
the road.
Some think it is east of us, others west of us.

Some say, "among primitive earth rocks," others, "in
the deep waters."

Kabir's instinct told him it was inside, and what it
was worth,
and he wrapped it up carefully in his heart cloth.

34

S wan, I'd like you to tell me your whole story!
Where you first appeared, and what dark sand
you are going toward,
and where you sleep at night, and what you are
looking for. . . .

It's morning, swan, wake up, climb in the air, follow
me!
I know of a country that spiritual flatness does not
control, nor constant depression,
and those alive are not afraid to die.
There wildflowers come up through the leafy floor,
and the fragrance of "I am he" floats on the wind.
There the bee of the heart stays deep inside the
flower,
and cares for no other thing.

35

Listen friend, this body is his dulcimer.
He draws the strings tight, and out of it comes
the music of the inner universe.
If the strings break and the bridge falls,
then this dulcimer of dust goes back to dust.

Kabir says: The Holy One is the only one who can
draw music from it.

36

Don't go outside your house to see flowers.
My friend, don't bother with that excursion.
Inside your body there are flowers.
One flower has a thousand petals.
That will do for a place to sit.
Sitting there you will have a glimpse of beauty
inside the body and out of it,
before gardens and after gardens.

48

37

The spiritual athlete often changes the color of his
clothes,
and his mind remains gray and loveless.

He sits inside a shrine room all day,
so that the Guest has to go outdoors and praise the
rocks.

Or he drills holes in his ears, his beard grows
enormous and matted,
people mistake him for a goat. . . .
He goes out into wilderness areas, strangles his
impulses,
and makes himself neither male nor female. . . .

He shaves his skull, puts his robe in an orange vat,
reads the Bhagavad-Gita, and becomes a terrific
talker.

Kabir says: Actually you are going in a hearse to the
country of death,
bound hand and foot!

38

Friend, please tell me what I can do about this world
I hold to, and keep spinning out!

I gave up sewn clothes, and wore a robe,
but I noticed one day the cloth was well woven.

So I bought some burlap, but I still
throw it elegantly over my left shoulder.

I pulled back my sexual longings,
and now I discover that I'm angry a lot.

I gave up rage, and now I notice
that I am greedy all day.

I worked hard at dissolving the greed,
and now I am proud of myself.

When the mind wants to break its link with the world
it still holds on to one thing.

Kabir says: Listen my friend,
there are very few that find the path!

39

The Holy One disguised as an old person
in a cheap hotel
goes out to ask for carfare.
But I never seem to catch sight of him.
If I did, what would I ask him for?
He has already experienced what is missing in my
life.
Kabir says: I belong to this old person.
Now let the events about to come, come!

40

At last the notes of his flute come in,
and I cannot stop from dancing around on the
floor. . . .

The blossoms open, even though it is not May,
and the bee knows of it already.

The air over the ocean is troubled,
there is a flash, heavy seas rise in my chest.

Rain pours down outside;
and inside I long for the Guest.

Something inside me has reached to the place
where the world is breathing.

The flags we cannot see are flying there.

Kabir says: My desire-body is dying, and it lives!

41

How hard it is to meet the Guest!
The rain bird is thirsty; she cries and whistles,
"Where is the rain?"
But she refuses all water but the rain. . . .

The deer comes out of her kind thickets when she
       hears music . . .
she does, she loves music,
and somehow knows she will die. . . .

The widow sits alone by her husband's body.
Soon the fire will be around her, and she is not
       afraid.
Don't have fears about his unimaginative body.

42

Have you heard the music that no fingers
enter into?
Far inside the house
entangled music —
What is the sense of leaving your house?

Suppose you scrub your ethical skin until it shines,
but inside there is no music,
then what?

Mohammed's son pores over words, and points out
    this
and that,
but if his chest is not soaked dark with love,
then what?

The Yogi comes along in his famous orange.
But if inside he is colorless, then what?

Kabir says: Every instant that the sun is risen,
    if I stand in the temple, or on a balcony,
    in the hot fields, or in a walled garden,
    my own Lord is making love with me.

43

The Guest is inside you, and also inside me;
you know the sprout is hidden inside the seed.
We are all struggling; none of us has gone far.
Let your arrogance go, and look around inside.

The blue sky opens out farther and farther,
the daily sense of failure goes away,
the damage I have done to myself fades,
a million suns come forward with light,
when I sit firmly in that world.

I hear bells ringing that no one has shaken,
inside "love" there is more joy than we know of,
rain pours down, although the sky is clear of clouds,
there are whole rivers of light.
The universe is shot through in all parts by a single
        sort of love.
How hard it is to feel that joy in all our four bodies!

Those who hope to be reasonable about it fail.
The arrogance of reason has separated us from that
        love.
With the word "reason" you already feel miles away.

How lucky Kabir is, that surrounded by all this joy
he sings inside his own little boat.
His poems amount to one soul meeting another.
These songs are about forgetting dying and loss.
They rise above both coming in and going out.

44

The woman who is separated from her lover
spins at the spinning wheel.

The Bagdad of the body rises with its towers and
    gates.
Inside it the palace of intelligence has been built.

The wheel of ecstatic love turns around in the sky,
and the spinning seat is made of the sapphires of
    work and study.

This woman weaves threads that are subtle,
and the intensity of her praise makes them fine!

Kabir says: I am that woman.
I am weaving the linen of night and day.

When my Lover comes and I feel his feet,
the gift I will have for him is tears.

Some Rumors About Kabir

1

No one knows much about Kabir. A few life details and a few stories are told over and over. He was evidently not a monk or ascetic, but was married, had children, and made his living by weaving cloth at home. Some say he was the son of Moslem parents, others that he was found on the streets and brought up by a Moslem couple. There may have been in the house books of the great Sufi poets of two hundred years before, such as Rumi. So it is possible Kabir knew the eccentric energy of the Sufis, the heretical or rebellious branch of the Mohammedans, by the time he was sixteen or seventeen. It is said he then asked Ramananda, the great Hindu ascetic, to initiate him. Ramananda had experienced the ecstatic power of the male god Rama, and took the name "the glad joy of Rama" as his name. Ramananda refused, saying, "No, you're a Moslem." Kabir knew which temple Ramananda meditated in each day before dawn, and Kabir lay down on the steps outside. Ramananda walked out in the half dark, and stepped on the boy's body. Astonished, he leaped up, and cried, "Rama!" Kabir then jumped up, and said, "You spoke the name of God in my presence. You initiated me. I'm your student!" Ramananda then, it is said, initiated him. Kabir became a powerful spiritual man and poet. His poems are amazing even in his wide tradition for the way he unites in one body the two rivers of ecstatic Sufism — supremely confident, secretive, desert meditation, utterly opposed to orthodoxy and academics, given to dance and weeping — and the Hindu tradition, which is more sober on the surface, coming through the Vedas and Vishnu, Ram, and Krishna.

Here's another Kabir story. At one time about fifteen hundred meditators came down from the hills and sat together in a big hall in north India. The number of people doing hard inner work in that century was large. They asked Kabir to read to them, but had not asked Mirabai. Mirabai composed ecstatic bhakti poems; her whole life flowed in the stream of Radha-Krishna intensity. She walked from village to village with holy men singing her poems "for the Dark One," and dancing; she was much loved. Kabir entered the hall, and said, "Where is Mirabai? You know what I see in this hall? I see fifteen hundred male egos." He refused to read until Mirabai came. So someone went for her — she was miles away — and they waited in silence, maybe one day or two. Mirabai at last arrived. She read for thirty-five minutes. At the end of that time it was clear that her bhakti was so much greater than anyone else's in the room, that the gathering broke up, and all the meditators, reminded of how much they had to do, went back to their huts.

Mirabai wrote her poems in Rajasthani, and about two hundred of them have survived. A later book in this Beacon Press series will include Mirabai poems. This story of Mirabai and Kabir is lovely, and as the Sufis would say, in the spiritual world it happened. In chronology there is a problem. When my first small group of Kabir versions was printed in Calcutta, the publisher set down firmly the birth date of Kabir as 1398, and the death date as 1518. That means he lived 120 years. That's possible. Most scholars guess Mirabai's birth date as 1498. That means Kabir was a hundred years old the day she was born. So if both dates are true, then she could have been 18 when she arrived at the hall, and he would have been 118 years old. That's possible; anything is possible. Or since dating is difficult, both birth dates may be wrong. We do know that both poets lived — accounts of people who met them have survived. Mirabai does mention Kabir in one of her poems, as well as another poet, Namdev, born earlier, around 1270. Mirabai says, speaking to Krishna:

> Oh you who lift mountains, stay with me always!
> You brought a full ox to Kabir's house,
>   and mended the hut where Namdev lived.

So there was a flow between the two, and the story suggests that very well.

2

Most of the observations a critic could make about Kabir's poems you can deduce by reading them. He does mention several times that his poems belong in the bhakti tradition, and I've decided to leave their word as it is. There's very little one can say about the bhakti tradition that doesn't diminish it. Perhaps we could see it more clearly by comparing it with a contrasting road. Some of the European saints of the Middle Ages, such as Tauler, walked the opposite path, they said no to the body and meant it. On this path the link between the ego and the body is emphasized, and the ego is then dispersed through humiliation of the body. The humiliation is a long process associated with hatred of the senses. The practicer tries to imagine how disgusting his or her body will be when it's dead, hair shirts and whips are used to humiliate the skin, attachments are dispersed, the practicer tries to free his spiritual energy from sexual energy by repulsion. Blake wrote the most powerful criticism of this path: "Better murder an infant in its cradle than nurse unacted desires." "Priests in black gowns are walking their rounds, and binding with briars my joys and desires." The road was called the "via negativa," and Eliot in his religious life consciously followed it.

The bhakti path is not peculiar to India, is no one's

invention, and I'm sure existed in Ras Shamra and among the Etruscans. Some of the Odin myths and Babylonian myths that seem to us quaint will be seen to refer to it. In the Indian subcontinent a vast rise of bhakti energy began in the eighth or ninth century, as if ocean water had suddenly reappeared in the center of a continent. Sometime during those centuries an alternative to the Vedic chanting began. The Vedas were in Sanskrit, and the chanting done for others by trained priests, by what we might call "religious academics." The new bhakti worship involved heart-love, feeling, dancing — Mirabai evidently used castanets and ankle rings — love of color, of intensity, of male-female poles, avoidance of convention, a discipline which is shared by Tristan and Isolde. Bhakti worship involves the present tense, and in contemporary language, rather than the old "classical" tongue, as when Dante decided to write *La Vita Nuova* in Italian rather than in Latin. The poets of India began to write ecstatic poetry in their local languages, and so refreshed the bhakti experience "from underneath." Some poems were written specifically for the long bhakti sessions, which lasted three or four hours in the middle of the night, and were guided through their stages by chanted and sung poems.

In north India, the bhakti experience became associated with Krishna as a visualization of the right side of the body, and Radha as a visualization of the left.

Jayadeva gave a great gift around 1200 with his *Gita Govinda,* and its ecstatic passages of Radha and Krishna lovemaking. "Great circle" dances appeared, and marvelous paintings, where Radha and Krishna look at each other with enormous eyes. "The joy of looking for him is so immense that you just dive in and coast around like a fish in the water. If anyone needs a head, the lover leaps up to offer his. Kabir's poems touch on the secrets of this bhakti." The male poets usually describe Radha and Krishna from outside, or evoke her feelings when separated. Mirabai never mentions Radha, just as Christ never mentions the Essenes, because he is the Essenes, just as she is Radha. Kabir sometimes speaks as a man, sometimes as a woman.

> This woman weaves threads that are subtle,
> and the intensity of her praise makes them fine.

> Kabir says: I am that woman.
> I am weaving the linen of night and day.

> When my lover comes and I feel his feet,
> the gift I will have for him is tears.

The ecstatic meditator, Shri Caitanya, traveled for a while around 1510–1530 from village to village in Bengal, teaching the villagers what bhakti experience looked and felt like, bringing dances with him, and the intensity rose higher. Namdev, Jnaneshwar, Chandidas, and Vidyapati wrote marvelous poems, all virtually unknown to us, in the years before Kabir. Mirabai, Kumbhandas, and Surdas are a few of the intense poets that followed.

3

Kabir in his joyful poems delivers harsh and unorthodox opinions. He enters controversies. For example, when Christ says, "The Kingdom of the Spirit resembles a cottonwood seed," the translators of the time found themselves dealing with three sets of opposites, familiar also to Chinese thought, of Spirit-Body, sky-earth, and Heaven–this world. The translator must choose among them. St. Paul, with other early fathers, committed the Church to translating the phrase as "the Kingdom of Heaven." The opposite state then is this life. Salvation is then driven into the next life. Kabir says a simple error of translation like this can destroy a religion. This throwing of intensity forward is a destructive habit of both Hindus and Moslems, and Kabir, attacking both, writes of that in his terrifying poem:

> If you don't break your ropes while you're alive,
> do you think ghosts
> will do it after?
>
> What is found now is found then
> If you find nothing now, you will simply end up
> with an apartment in the city of death.

The best known religious poetry in English, of Vaughn

and Traherne, for example, contains rather mild and orthodox ideas. Such harsh instruction as Kabir gives we are unprepared for. In Vaughn the thought and feeling swim together under the shelter of a gentle dogma. In Kabir one leaps ahead of the other, as if jumping out of the sea, and the reader smiles in joy at so much energy. It is as if both thought and feeling fed a third thing, a rebellious originality, and with that tail the poem shoots through the water. We feel that speed sometimes in Eckhart also. Kabir says that when you work in interior work, the work is not done by the method, but by the intensity. "Look at me, and you will see a slave of that intensity." The word "intensity" widens to its full range here. We understand that such intensity is impossible without having intense feeling, intense thinking, intense intuition, and intense love of colors and odors and animals. He hears the sound of "the anklets on the feet of an insect as it walks."

In Kabir's poems then you see the astonishing event — highly religious and intensely spiritual poems written outside of, and in opposition to, the standard Hindu, Mohammedan, or Christian dogmas. Kabir says, "Suppose you scrub your ethical skin until it shines, but inside there is no music, then what?" He also attacks the simple-minded Yoga practices and guru cults, such as we see growing up all around us in the United States. It's valuable to have these practices discussed by an Indian, not a Westerner. Kabir says, "The Yogi comes along in his famous orange. But if inside he is colorless, then what?" To Kabir, the main danger is spiritual passivity. Kabir is opposed to repeating any truth from another teacher, whether of English literature or Buddhism, that you yourself have not experienced.

> The Sacred Books of the East are nothing but words.
> I looked through their covers one day sideways.
>
> Kabir talks only about what he has lived through.
> If you have not lived through something, it is not true.

Kabir mocks passivity toward holy texts, toward popular gurus, and the passive practice of Yoga, but we must understand that he himself is firmly in the guru tradition and that he followed an intricate path, with fierce meditative practices, guided by energetic visualizations of "sun" and "moon" energies. In poems not translated here — I don't have the language for it, nor the experience — he dives into the whole matter of Sakti energy, ways of uniting right and left, and going upward with "the third". . . . These labors have not been experienced yet in the West, or have been experienced, but discussed at length only in alchemy. He has, moreover, enigmatic or puzzle poems that no contemporary commentator fully understands. I love his poems, and am grateful every day for their gift.

Robert Bly

We are deeply indebted to the following persons and organizations for permission to reproduce art from their collections:

The illustrations on page xii (Krishna with the Flute, 17th or early 18th century; Jamū, Pahārī, Rajput, Ross Coomaraswamy Collection); page 18 (Siva and Pāravatī; Indian, Paper .213 x 1295 m., Ross Coomaraswamy Collection); and page 54 (Upapātī Nateka, "The Paramour Gallant," Late 17th century; Basholi, Pāharī, Rajput, Ross Coomaraswamy Collection) appear courtesy of the Museum of Fine Arts, Boston. The illustrations on page 12 (Krishna Fluting, Malwa, 18th century) and page 16 (a Mihrab in Kufic script, Deccan, Hyderabad, ca. 1800), courtesy of a private collection. Illustrations on pages 26, 30, and 34 (Charkra paintings, from Philip Rawson, *The Art of Tantra*, Thames and Hudson, 1973) are reproduced from the Collection Ajit Mookerjee, New Delhi. The illustration on page 48 (album painting, representing the terrible Goddess Kālī, Rājasthān, 18th century), Crown Copyright, Victoria and Albert Museum, London.

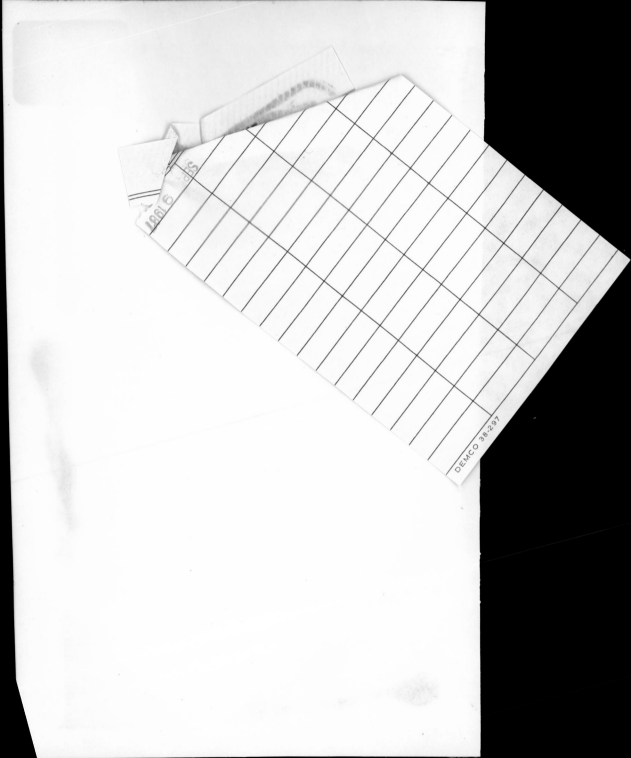